Read These Too

Snowballs in the Bookdrop
(W.M., 1982)

Bibliotoons
(G.H., McFarland, 1990)

Unintellectual Freedoms
(W.M., McFarland, 1991)

Unprofessional Behavior
(W.M. & G.H., McFarland, 1992)

Unsolicited Advice
(W.M. & G.H., McFarland, 1992)

For Library Directors Only
(W.M. & R. Lee, McFarland, 1993)

For Library Trustees Only
(W.M. & R. Lee, McFarland, 1993)

The Manley Art of Librarianship
(W.M., McFarland, 1993)